PIANO

Adventures® *by Nancy and Randall Faber*

THE BASIC PIANO METHOD

CONTENTS

A triad is a 3-note chord built in 3rds.

- The three notes of a triad are the **root**, **3rd**, and **5th**.
- All major and minor chords and their inversions are triads.
- The **primary triads** in any key are the **I**, **IV**, and **V** chords.
  (In a minor key, lower case **i** and **iv** indicate minor chords.)

Triad

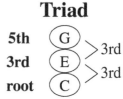

5th   G
3rd   E   } 3rd
root   C   } 3rd

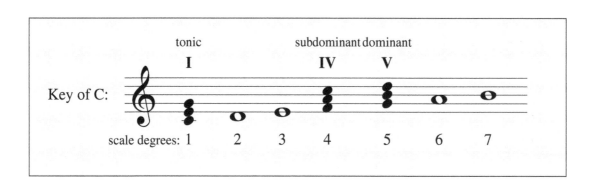

Key of C:

tonic   subdominant dominant

I   IV   V

scale degrees: 1   2   3   4   5   6   7

Triad Trainer

1. Notice the key. Then circle the correct answer for each triad: **tonic, subdominant,** or **dominant.**

Key of G Major

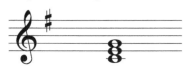

Ex. tonic (**I**)

~~subdominant (**IV**)~~ ⭕

dominant (**V**)

Key of D Major

tonic (**I**)

subdominant (**IV**)

dominant (**V**)

Key of A minor

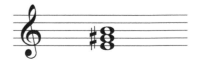

tonic (**i**)

subdominant (**iv**)

dominant (**V**)

Key of E Major

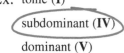

tonic (**I**)

subdominant (**IV**)

dominant (**V**)

Key of F Major

tonic (**I**)

subdominant (**IV**)

dominant (**V**)

Key of A Major

tonic (**I**)

subdominant (**IV**)

dominant (**V**)

Key of G Major

tonic (**I**)

subdominant (**IV**)

dominant (**V**)

Key of D minor

tonic (**i**)

subdominant (**iv**)

dominant (**V**)

Key of E minor

tonic (**i**)

subdominant (**iv**)

dominant (**V**)

Lessons p. 6

FF1094

Chord Inversion Review:

Major and minor triads have 3 positions: **root position, 1st inversion,** and **2nd inversion.**

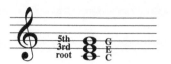

Root position

The root (chord name)
is on the bottom.

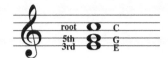

1st inversion

The 3rd is on the bottom.

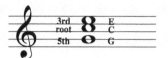

2nd inversion

The 5th is on the bottom.

2. Complete the chord inversion puzzle by spelling **root position**, **1st inversion**, or **2nd inversion triads**.

ACROSS →

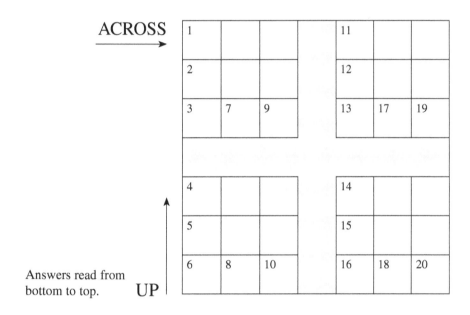

Answers read from
bottom to top.   UP

Chord Inversion Puzzle

ACROSS	**UP**
1. C major, root position	3. C major, 1st inversion
2. C major, 2nd inversion	6. D major, root position
3. C major, 1st inversion	7. C major, 2nd inversion
4. F major, 1st inversion	8. F major, root position
5. D major, 1st inversion *(Remember the sharp.)*	9. C major, root position
6. D minor, root position	10. D minor, 2nd inversion
11. E minor, root position	13. C major, 2nd inversion
12. C minor, root position *(Remember the flat.)*	16. F minor, 1st inversion *(Remember the flat.)*
13. G minor, root position	17. E♭ major, 2nd inversion *(Remember the flats.)*
14. D minor, 1st inversion	18. F major, 2nd inversion
15. F major, 2nd inversion	19. G major, 2nd inversion
16. F minor, 1st inversion *(Remember the flat.)*	20. D minor, 1st inversion

Extra Credit: Can you play each of the triads shown ACROSS on the puzzle?
Name the triad and its position: **root position**, **1st inversion**, or **2nd inversion**.

Lessons p. 6

A **cadence** is a progression of chords that leads to a
natural resting or "breathing" point in the music.

- A cadence occurs at the end of a phrase, section, or piece.
- Cadences usually end on a **I** or a **V** (or V7) chord.

3. *Vivace* has 4 cadences.
- Write **I** or **V** in the boxes to show the harmony of each cadence.
- Then sightread the piece at a moderate tempo. *Listen* for the cadences.

Vivace

Cornelius Gurlitt
(1820-1901, Germany)
original form

cadence on? ☐

☐ to ☐

cadence on? ☐

☐ to ☐

4

Compound Meter

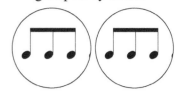

When the **top number** of a time signature can be divided by 3, the beats are grouped into 3's. This is known as *compound meter*.

For example: $\frac{6}{8} = 3+3$ $\frac{9}{8} = 3+3+3$ $\frac{12}{8} = 3+3+3+3$

In compound meter, it is often easier to feel and count the **main beats** in the measure. The main beats can be called **pulses**.

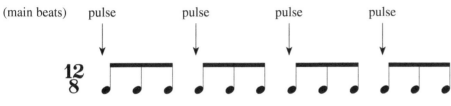

4. Clap and count: **1** and a **2** and a **3** and a **4** and a

4 groups of 3 = 12!

5. For each rhythm below:

- Circle each group of 3 beats.
- Mark 4 PULSES per measure with an ↓ arrow.
- Play and count aloud, "**1** and a **2** and a **3** and a **4** and a."

a.

Transpose to a D major triad.

b.

Transpose to an F major triad.

6. Write one measure of your own rhythm in $\frac{12}{8}$ time. Choose from the rhythm patterns shown.

one measure

$\frac{12}{8}$

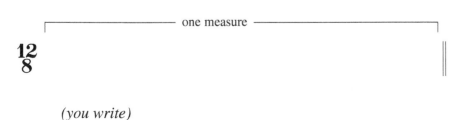

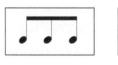

(you write)

Harmony Warm-up:

7. Draw **triads** on scale degrees **1, 4,** and **5** of the E major scale below.
Then play each triad, saying aloud "**tonic**," "**subdominant**," or "**dominant**."

8. a. Write **I**, **IV**, or **V** in each box to show the harmony.

b. Compose your own **R.H. melody** using the rhythm
suggested. Write your melody on the staff.

Hint: Find melody notes that sound pleasing
with the L.H. accompaniment.

c. Play *New River Etude* with pedal.

New River Etude

(Your own composition)

Ex. **I**

FF1094

Lessons p. 14

9. These melodies use different **accompaniment patterns**.

Sightread each example. Then transpose to the keys suggested.

Broken octaves

Allegretto

Transpose to D major.

Waltz bass

Moderato

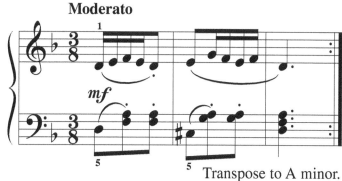

Transpose to A minor.

Arpeggios

Lento

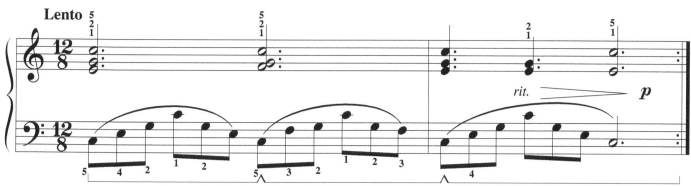

rit. *p*

Transpose to G major.

10. Your teacher will play a **cadence**.

Listen! Circle **I** or **V7** for the LAST harmony that you hear.

Hint: The **I** chord sounds *restful*. The **V7** chord sounds *restless*.

a. **I**
or
V7

b. **I**
or
V7

c. **I**
or
V7

d. **I**
or
V7

For Teacher Use Only (The examples may be played in any order and repeated several times.)

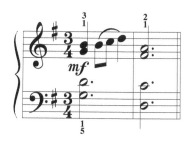   

7

Perfect Intervals (4th, 5th, octave)

To measure an interval, use a major scale (or major 5-finger pattern) beginning on the *lower* note.

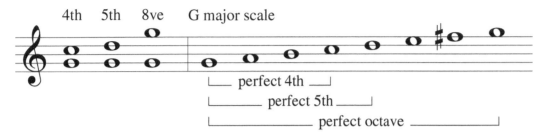

4ths, 5ths, and octaves are called *perfect* intervals.* They are neither major nor minor.

1. Play and *listen* to these perfect intervals. (**P** for **perfect**)

P4

Think: D major scale or
5-finger pattern
(A perfect 4th = 5 half steps)

P5

Think: E major scale or
5-finger pattern
(A perfect 5th = 7 half steps)

P8 (octave)

Think: same letter name
(A perfect octave = 12 half steps)

Tritone Alert: The interval of a tritone spans **3 whole steps**.

Once known as the *diabolus in musica* (devil in music), it is neither perfect, major, nor minor.

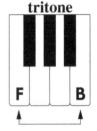

tritone

F   B

2. Find and play several tritones. *Listen* to the unusual sound!

3. Draw a whole note to complete each **perfect interval** below. Then play, naming each interval aloud. *Listen* to the sound.

Perfect in Every Way

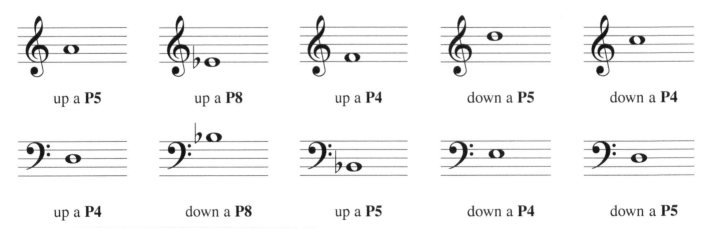

up a **P5**   up a **P8**   up a **P4**   down a **P5**   down a **P4**

up a **P4**   down a **P8**   up a **P5**   down a **P4**   down a **P5**

*Note: A perfect interval inverts to a perfect interval. For example, a **P4** (D to G) inverts to a **P5** (G to D). Each note is included in the major scale of the other.

Lesson: p. 18

FF109

Composing with 4ths

4. a. Write **perfect 4ths** moving UP from bass C. **Use half notes.** Notice the flats!
(Hint: The last chord uses all the 4ths you have written.)

b. Now play, holding the damper pedal down.
Listen to the majestic sound of perfect 4ths!

Fanfare of 4ths

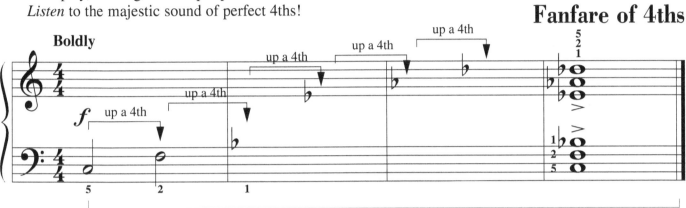

c. **Create your own** *Fanfare of 4ths.* Have fun using the suggestions below.
 • Repeat any note using a rhythm of your choice.
 • Play the 4ths *ascending* (going up) and *descending* (going down).
 • Play the last chord *forte,* moving up in octaves.

Composing with 5ths

5. a. Write **perfect 5ths** for the right hand, coming DOWN the keyboard. **Use half notes.**
Tritone Alert: Avoid the **B-F** tritone.

b. Hold the damper pedal down as you play your "Ocean Sunset."
Listen to the peaceful sound of perfect 5ths.

Ocean Sunset

c. **Create a longer version of** *Ocean Sunset.* Here are some suggestions:
 • Play the notes of each 5th separately (called **melodic 5ths.**)
 • Repeat any 5th using a rhythm of your choice.
 • Explore different dynamics: *pp   p   mp   mf   f   ff*

6.  Do Ear-training DRILL 1 on p. 16 using **perfect 4ths**, **5ths**, and **octaves**.

Lessons p. 19

Major and Minor 2nds and 3rds

The intervals of a **2nd** and **3rd** can be either major or minor.

1. Play these intervals, naming them aloud. *Listen* to the sound! (**M** = major; **m** = minor)

m2	**M2**	**m3**	**M3**
half step	whole step	whole step + half step (3 half steps)	2 whole steps (4 half steps)

Brain Teasers

2. Challenge yourself with these "brain teasers." You may use a keyboard to help you.

a. True or False *(circle)* "All **major 3rds** are from a *white key* to a *white key*."

b. Give 3 examples which disprove the above statement. ___ to ___; ___ to ___; ___ to ___

c. True or False *(circle)* "All **minor 3rds** include a black key."

d. Give 3 examples which disprove the above statement. ___ to ___; ___ to ___; ___ to ___

e. Name the **M3** that is from a *black key* to a *black key.* ___ to ___

f. Name a **m3** that is from a *black key* to a *black key.* ___ to ___

g. The *root* to the *3rd* of a **major triad** is the interval of a **major 3rd**.
   What interval is formed by the *3rd* to the *5th* of a major triad? _____

h. What interval is formed by the *3rd* to the *5th* of a **minor triad**? _____

i. Identify the following intervals (**m2, M2, m3,** or **M3**).

Brain Bruiser: Name the note that is a **M3** below E♭? _____
(Caution: A 3rd must be spelled to span 3 letter names.)

3. Do Ear-training DRILL 2 on p. 16 using **major & minor 2nds** and **3rds**.

Composing with 2nds and 3rds

Complete these short compositions by writing the correct **intervals** on the staffs.
Then play the music. Create a "sound picture" of the title.

4. a. Write a **major 2nd** either UP or DOWN from the note given
      to complete each measure. **Use half notes.**

   b. Play using the damper pedal. *Listen* to the sound of major 2nds!

Fog at Midnight

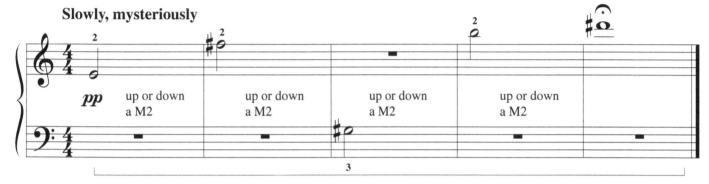

5. a. Write a **minor 2nd** either UP or DOWN from the note given
      to complete each measure. **Use staccato quarter notes.**

   b. Play and *listen* to the sound of minor 2nds!

Suspense Theater

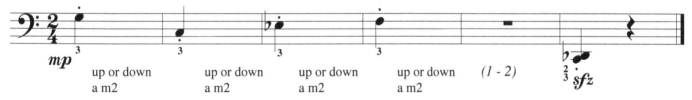

6. a. Write **major 3rds** or **minor 3rds** moving UP the keyboard
      to complete each measure. **Use dotted half notes.**

   b. Write **M3** or **m3** in the blank above each measure.
      Then play with pedal. (Change pedal as needed.)

Tropical Island

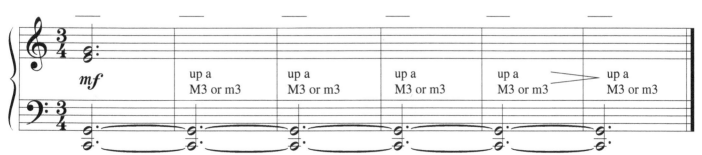

Lessons p. 19

Major and Minor 6ths

Think of a **M6** (major 6th) as a **perfect 5th plus a whole step**.

Think of a **m6** (minor 6th) as a **perfect 5th plus a half step**.

1. a. Play this **M6** and *listen* to the sound.

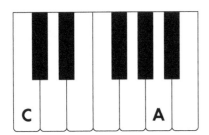

b. Play this **m6** and *listen* to the sound.

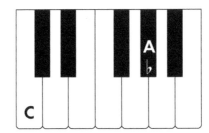

The Empire 6th Building

2. Take the elevator UP to the top floor. Move by **major** or **minor 6ths** as directed. Write the **letter name** on the correct keys. Did you land at the telescope on the roof?

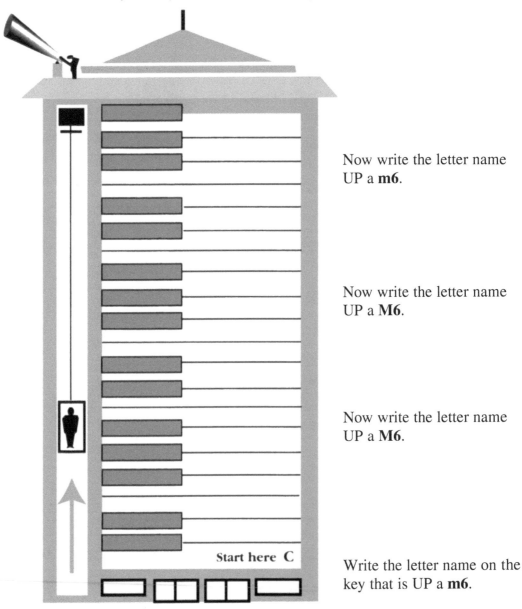

Now write the letter name UP a **m6**.

Now write the letter name UP a **M6**.

Now write the letter name UP a **M6**.

Write the letter name on the key that is UP a **m6**.

Start here C

**3.** Do Ear-training DRILL 3 on p. 16 using **major** and **minor 6ths**.

FF1094

Lessons p. 19

Composing with 6ths

4. Compose your own piece using **6ths**. Follow these guidelines:

- **Write 6ths for the R.H. using only white keys.**
  Follow the rhythm suggested.

- Give your piece a title, and play it using pedal.
  Listen to the pleasing sound of 6ths!

_____
(title)

Extra Credit: Your teacher may ask you to identify each 6th you have written as a **major** or **minor 6th**.

Lessons p. 19

Major and Minor 7ths

Think of a **M7** (major 7th) as a
HALF STEP smaller than an octave.

Think of a **m7** (minor 7th) as a
WHOLE STEP smaller than an octave.

1. a. Play this **M7** and *listen* to the sound.

b. Play this **m7** and *listen* to the sound.

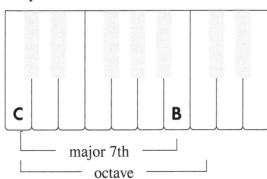

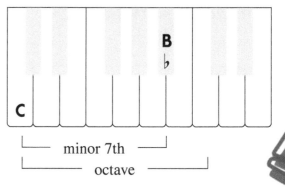

2. Write the correct letter name on each keyboard
to complete the **major** or **minor 7th**.

Seventh Search

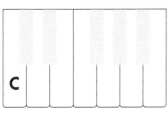

up a Major 7th

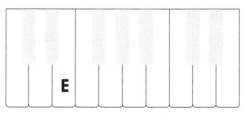

up a minor 7th

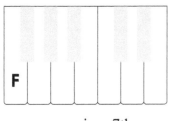

up a minor 7th

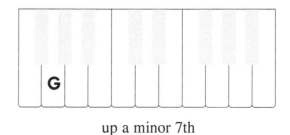

up a minor 7th

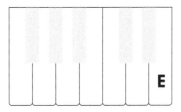

down a Major 7th

down a minor 7th

3. Write a **major 7th** or **minor 7th** on the staves below.

up a **m7**   up a **M7**   up a **m7**   down a **M7**   down a **m7**

4. Do Ear-training DRILL 4 on p. 16 using **major** and **minor 7ths**.

FF1094

Lessons p. 19

Sightreading Tips

1. First notice the **key signature** and **time signature**.

2. Scan the music for:
   - **rhythm patterns** (repeated rhythms)
   - **harmony patterns** (especially L.H. chords and intervals)
   - **melody patterns** (repetition and sequence)

3. Set a rather slow tempo. Count one "free" measure before beginning.

4. Keep your eyes moving ahead.
   Don't stop to correct mistakes when sightreading!

5. Sightread each musical example. Then transpose to the keys suggested.

Key of ____ major

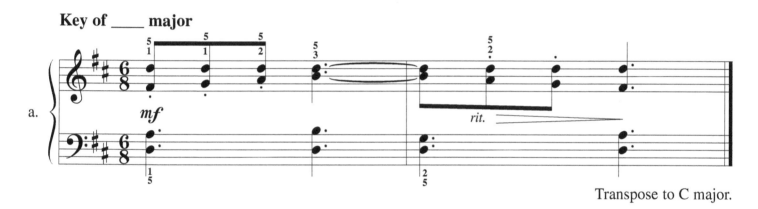

a.

Transpose to C major.

Key of ____ major

b.

Transpose to F major.

Key of ____ major

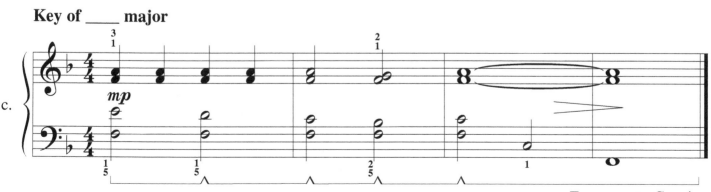

c.

Transpose to G major.

Lessons p. 19

Your teacher will drill you on **interval recognition** over many lessons.

"Warm up" your ears by working with just one ear-training drill at a time. Later, try combining several drills for an ear-training challenge.

Teacher Directions: Choose the notes for each interval from the middle range of the keyboard. Play the notes of the intervals separately (ascending), then together. (Some teachers and students may wish to sing the pitches.)

Drill 1	Perfect 4ths, 5ths, and octaves

Listening Hints: Examples:

- a **4th** sounds like
  Here Comes the Bride

- a **5th** sounds like the
  opening to *Twinkle,
  Twinkle* or *Scarborough Fair*

- an **octave** sounds like the
  opening to *Somewhere
  Over the Rainbow,* or
  I'm Singin' in the Rain

Drill 2	Major & minor 2nds and 3rds

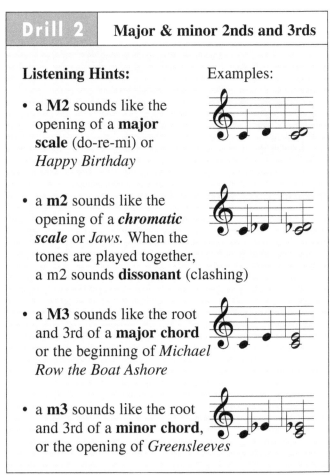

Listening Hints: Examples:

- a **M2** sounds like the
  opening of a **major
  scale** (do-re-mi) or
  Happy Birthday

- a **m2** sounds like the
  opening of a **chromatic
  scale** or *Jaws.* When the
  tones are played together,
  a m2 sounds **dissonant** (clashing)

- a **M3** sounds like the root
  and 3rd of a **major chord**
  or the beginning of *Michael
  Row the Boat Ashore*

- a **m3** sounds like the root
  and 3rd of a **minor chord**,
  or the opening of *Greensleeves*

Drill 3	Major & minor 6ths

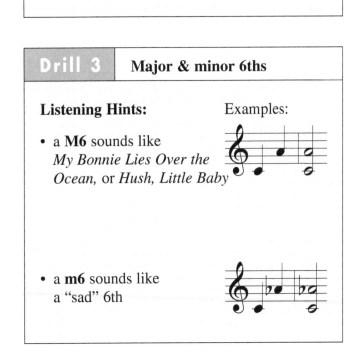

Listening Hints: Examples:

- a **M6** sounds like
  *My Bonnie Lies Over the
  Ocean,* or *Hush, Little Baby*

- a **m6** sounds like
  a "sad" 6th

Drill 4	Major & minor 7ths

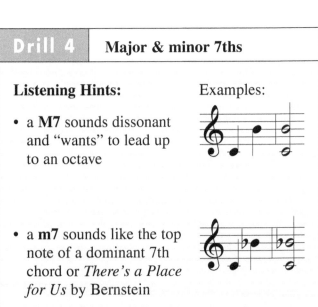

Listening Hints: Examples:

- a **M7** sounds dissonant
  and "wants" to lead up
  to an octave

- a **m7** sounds like the top
  note of a dominant 7th
  chord or *There's a Place
  for Us* by Bernstein

Lessons p. 19

16

FF1094

The Circle of 5ths

The circle of 5ths will help you learn scales and key signatures.

- For flat keys, circle to the left, moving DOWN by **perfect 5ths**.

- For sharp keys, circle to the right, moving UP by **perfect 5ths**.

1. Name each key signature around the circle of 5ths.

Then write the **tonic chord** for each key on the staff provided.

The last sharp is the *leading tone*.

The next to the last flat is the key name.
(F is an exception.)

Go up a half step from the last sharp for the key name.

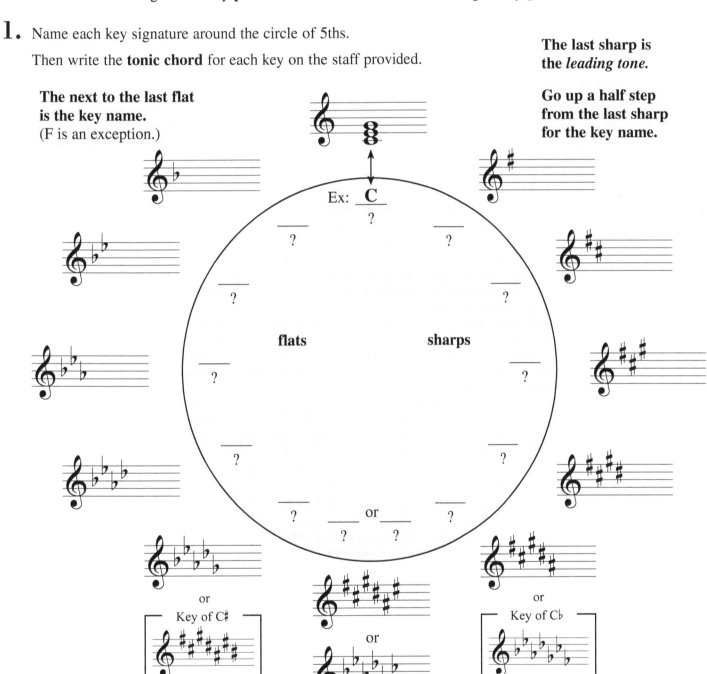

2. Play and memorize these patterns. It will help you remember sharp and flat **key signatures**.

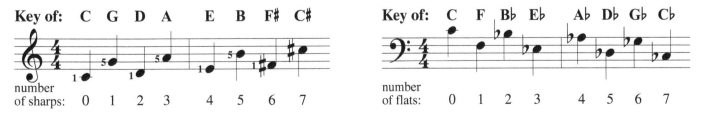

The 3 "building blocks" of music are: **RHYTHM, MELODY,** and **HARMONY.**

3. Composing with the Circle of 5ths

Harmony: Play the left hand alone several times.
Notice the harmony is based on the **circle of 5ths**.

Rhythm: Choose any key and play the rhythm shown by the cue notes.

Melody: Compose a right-hand melody using the rhythm of the cue notes.

Hint: First experiment by finding melody notes that sound
pleasing with the left hand, such as **chord tones** (root-3rd-5th).

Lastly, practice your composition for an artistic performance.
Yes, composers have to practice their own music!

_____
(your title)

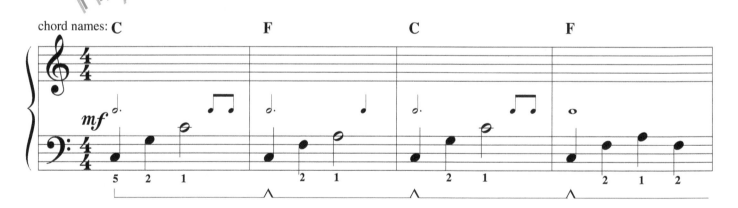

Suggestion: For *measures 5-8,* write a **sequence** of *measures 1-4.*
(This will give your melody continuity.)

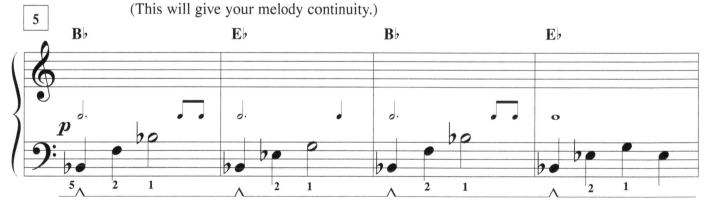

18

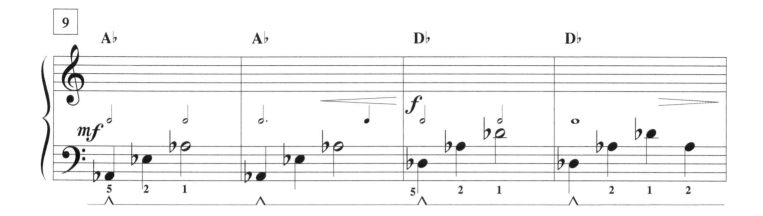

Suggestion: For *measures 13-16,* write an **exact repeat** of *measures 9-12,*
or write your melody **one octave higher**.

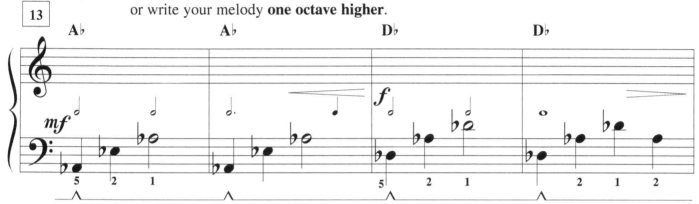

Suggestion: For *measures 17-20,* **return** to the melody of *measures 1-4.*
Notice the chord pattern is the same.

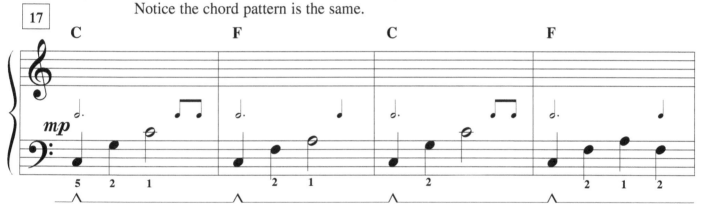

Codetta (short ending)

Use this codetta, or create your own based on **C broken chords**.

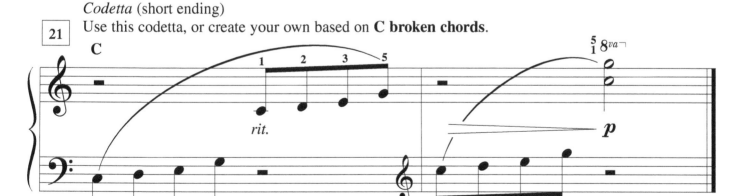

Congratulations, composer!

Extra Credit: Have a friend "double" your melody on flute, violin, or digital keyboard.

4. Write the **chord letter names** in the boxes. Notice the **circle of 5ths** movement.

Then sightread the music at a slow tempo.

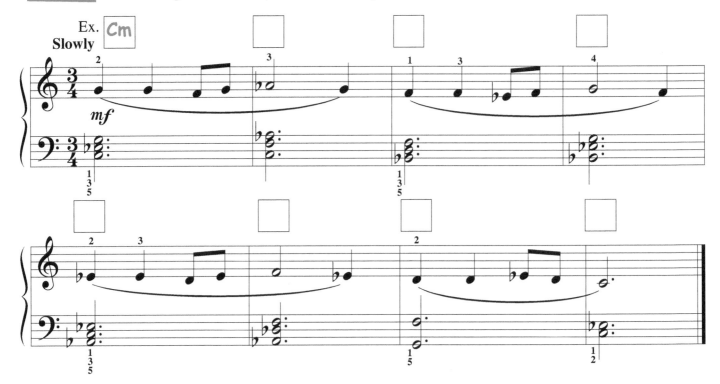

5. Each example follows the **circle of 5ths** (counter-clockwise).

Listen to the movement of the **bass notes** (lowest notes).

Circle the *last* chord you hear.

1. **C   F   B♭   E♭   A♭**   2. **C   F   B♭   E♭   A♭**

3. **C   F   B♭   E♭   A♭**   4. **C   F   B♭   E♭   A♭**

For Teacher Use Only (The examples may be played in any order and repeated several times.)

Hint: Emphasize the bass notes when playing.

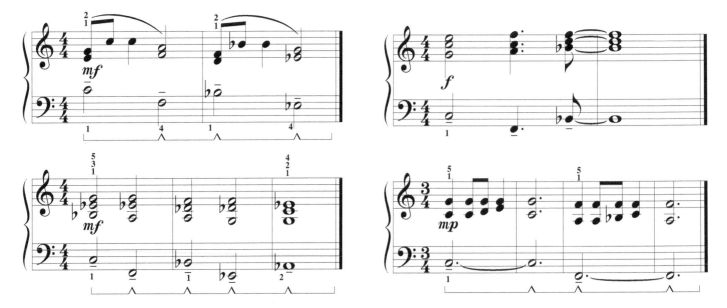

FF109

Arpeggio means "harp-like."

For an arpeggio, play **chord tones** (the notes of a chord)
one after another, moving up or down the keyboard.

Arpeggio Hunt

1. Show an *arpeggio* by putting an "✗" on all **chord tones** going UP the keyboard.
Then name the arpeggio in the blank to the right.

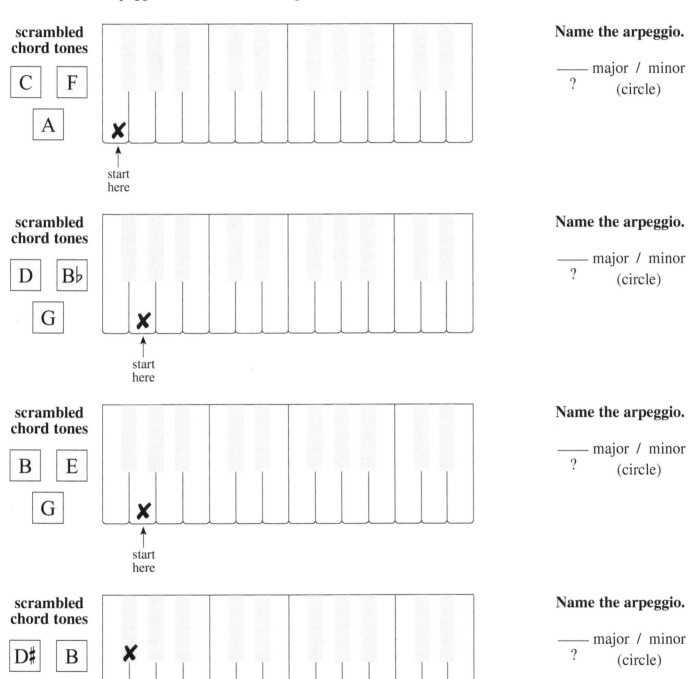

scrambled
chord tones

C   F

A

Name the arpeggio.

—— major / minor
? (circle)

scrambled
chord tones

D   B♭

G

Name the arpeggio.

—— major / minor
? (circle)

scrambled
chord tones

B   E

G

Name the arpeggio.

—— major / minor
? (circle)

scrambled
chord tones

D♯   B

F♯

Name the arpeggio.

—— major / minor
? (circle)

start here (under each keyboard)

Extra Credit: Play the arpeggios above with R.H., then L.H.
Begin on the **root of each chord** and play two octaves up and down.
Use pedal and *listen* to the chord tones blend.

Lessons p. 26

Left-Hand Arpeggio Study

2. a. Write the **missing chord tones** to complete the left-hand arpeggios.

b. Write the correct **L.H. fingering** in the blanks.

c. Write a **tempo mark** and **metronome mark** of your choice.

d. Practice and perform *Harp Etude* **using pedal**. (Change the pedal for each new harmony as indicated.)

Harp Etude

FF1C

Arpeggiated or Rolled Chord:

Play the notes *quickly,* bottom to top.

3. First, write the **chord letter name** for each arpeggiated (rolled) chord.

Then sightread at an *andante* tempo.

Hint: Hold each note as it is played. Begin the R.H. *after* the L.H. notes.

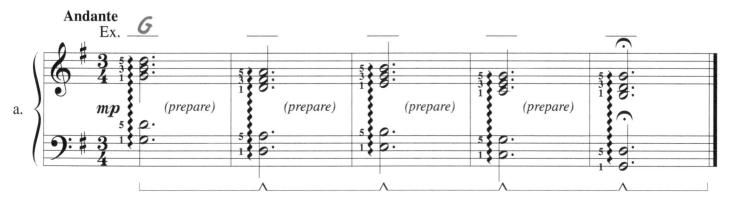

Andante
Ex. G

a.

Write the chord name for each **right-hand arpeggio**. Then sightread at a slow blues tempo.

Slow Blues   Ex. D

b.

5

4. Your teacher will play a two-octave arpeggio or a rolled chord.

Listen, then circle **major** or **minor** for the sound you hear.

1. **major** or **minor**   2. **major** or **minor**   3. **major** or **minor**   4. **major** or **minor**

Note: The teacher should continue the drill, playing more major and minor arpeggios for the student to identify.

Lessons p. 30

094

23

Naming Flat Key Signatures

For flat key signatures, the **next to the last flat** is the name of the key.

Ex.

Eb is the next to the last flat.

Eb is the name of the key.

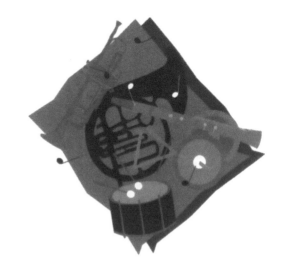

Famous Marches

1. Below are the opening melodies to famous marches.

Name the **key signature** for each instrumental part below.

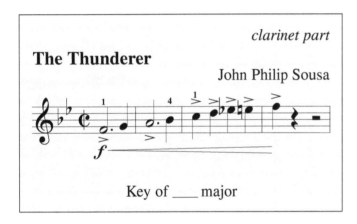

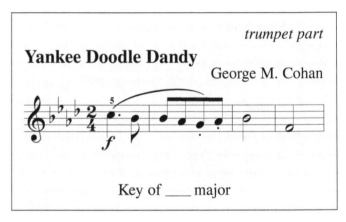

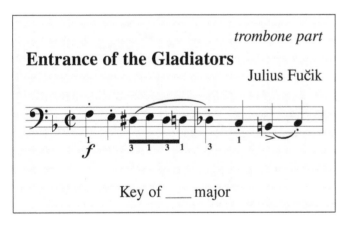

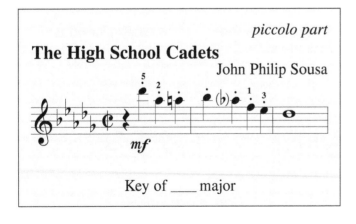

The Flat Pattern

The pattern of flats is always written the same.

The complete flat pattern has 7 flats:

spells "bead"

Bb Eb Ab Db Gb Cb Fb

Notice the flats move **down by 5ths** (counterclockwise around the circle of 5ths.)

2. Study these rules and examples:

- Always begin with Bb.
- Continue the pattern, moving **up a 4th** and **down a 5th**.

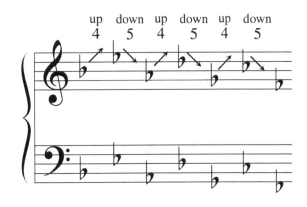

3. How fast can you write the **flat pattern** in both clefs?
Have your teacher, parent, or friend time you.

In No Time Flat!

_____ seconds   _____ seconds   _____ seconds

4. Write the flat key signatures below.

Hint: Begin writing the flat pattern. Continue the pattern until you have drawn **one flat beyond the name of the key**.

Check yourself! The key name should always be the next-to-the-last flat. (F is the exception.)

Bb major   **Ab major**   **Eb major**   **Db major**

one flat past
the key name

Ex.

key name

Eb major   **F major**   **Ab major**   **Gb major**

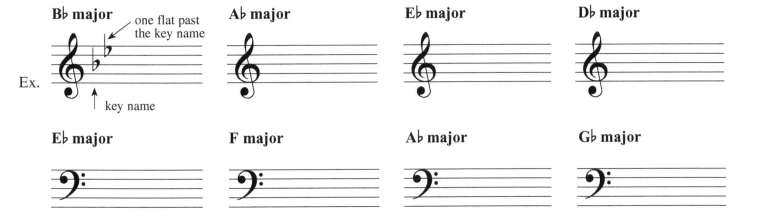

The Two Positions for R.H. Flat Scales

Flat scales for the R.H. can be quickly learned using these two finger positions.

- **R.H. fingers 1-2-3** relate to the 2-black key group. **Thumb plays on C.**
- **R.H. fingers 1-2-3-4** relate to the 3-black key group. **Thumb plays on F.**

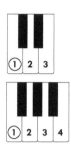

Genius Fingers
(for R.H.)

5. Play these right-hand finger patterns for each key.
Your thumb always plays on C and F!

Notice where the flats fall, and how your fingers *feel* for each flat scale.

Play the positions several times. Then play a
two-octave scale beginning on the **tonic of each key**.

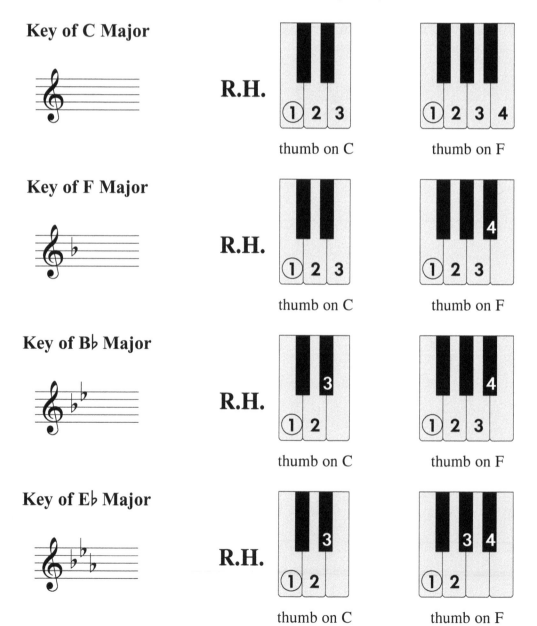

Key of C Major

R.H.

thumb on C   thumb on F

Key of F Major

R.H.

thumb on C   thumb on F

Key of B♭ Major

R.H.

thumb on C   thumb on F

Key of E♭ Major

R.H.

thumb on C   thumb on F

26

FF1

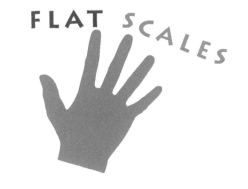

Playing R.H. Flat Scales

6. Write the R.H. fingering for each scale below.
- First, write **1** (thumb) for every **C and F**. Circle each **1**.
- Then complete the scale fingering by filling in the blanks.

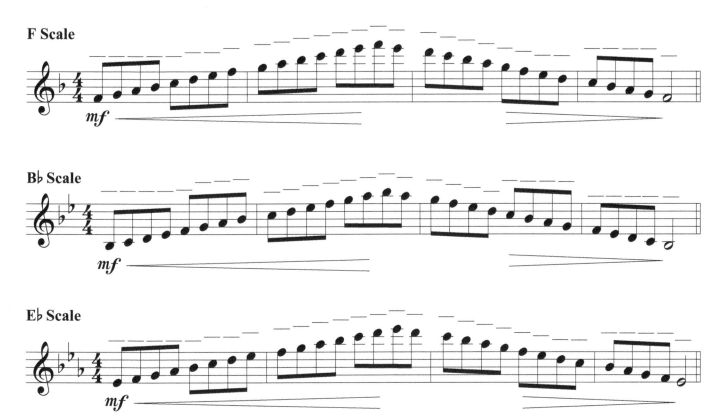

F Scale

B♭ Scale

E♭ Scale

Extra Credit: Can you play each R.H. scale from memory?
Play each scale *legato,* then *staccato.*

Playing L.H. Flat Scales

The B♭ and E♭ left-hand scales use this finger pattern:

L.H. | 3 - 2 - 1 | plus | 4 - 3 - 2 - 1 |

7. Draw a box around these finger patterns for the scales below.

Extra Credit: Can you play each L.H. scale up and down from memory? Say the finger pattern aloud.
Play each scale *legato,* then *staccato.*

Lessons p. 33

The B♭ Major Scale

8. Write the key signature for **B♭ major**.
Then write the B♭ major scale using whole notes.
Shade in the flatted notes.

The Ski Slope

9. Fill in the correct answer for
each location on the mountain.

The
tonic in
B♭ is _____

The **leading tone**
(scale degree 7)
in B♭ is _____

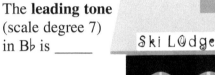

Scale degree 6
in B♭ is _____

Name the notes of
the **V7** chord in B♭.

_____ _____ _____ _____
root   3rd   5th   7th

The **dominant**
(scale degree 5)
in B♭ is _____

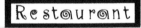

The **subdominant**
(scale degree 4)
in B♭ is _____

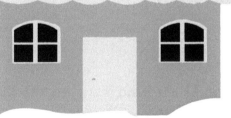

Scale degree 3
in B♭ is _____

Name the notes of
the **IV** chord in B♭.

_____ _____ _____
root   3rd   5th

Scale degree 2
in B♭ is _____

The **tonic**
(scale degree 1)
in B♭ is _____

Name the notes of
the **I** chord in B♭.

_____ _____ _____
root   3rd   5th

Chord Analysis in B♭ Major

10. Analyze the harmony of this piece by doing the following:

- Write the **chord letter name** in the blank above each measure.
- Write the **Roman numeral I, IV,** or **V7** in the boxes below.

Then play *Taxicab Blues* using swing rhythm.

Taxicab Blues

Lessons p. 38

Test Your Knowledge in E♭ Major

11. Test your knowledge of the **key of E♭ major** by completing each box.

Write the **key signature** for E♭ in both clefs.

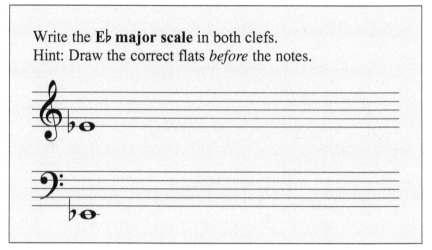

Write the **E♭ major scale** in both clefs.
Hint: Draw the correct flats *before* the notes.

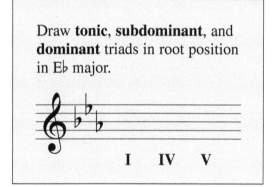

Draw **tonic**, **subdominant**, and **dominant** triads in root position in E♭ major.

       I   **IV**   **V**

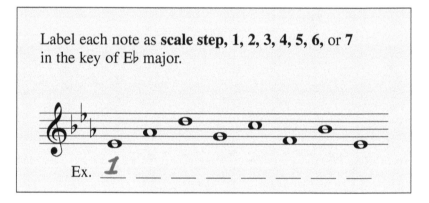

Label each note as **scale step, 1, 2, 3, 4, 5, 6,** or **7** in the key of E♭ major.

Ex. *1* ___ ___ ___ ___ ___ ___ ___

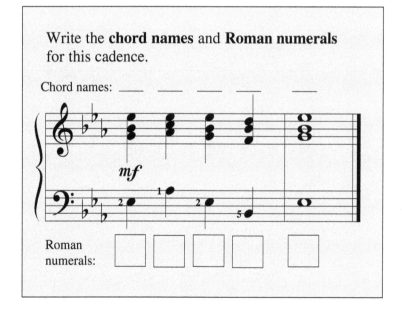

Write the **chord names** and **Roman numerals** for this cadence.

Chord names: ___ ___ ___ ___ ___

Roman numerals:

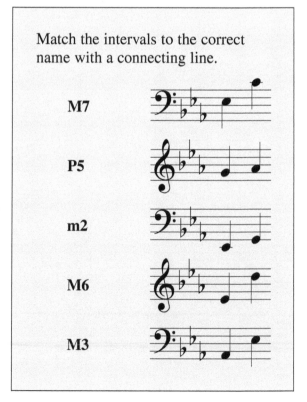

Match the intervals to the correct name with a connecting line.

M7

P5

m2

M6

M3

Extra Credit: Play the musical examples on this page for your teacher.

FF1

Alberti Bass Review:

The Alberti bass is this L.H. accompaniment pattern: *bottom - top - middle - top*

12. Play the Alberti bass pattern using **I**, **IV**, and **V7** chords in the key of **E♭ major**.

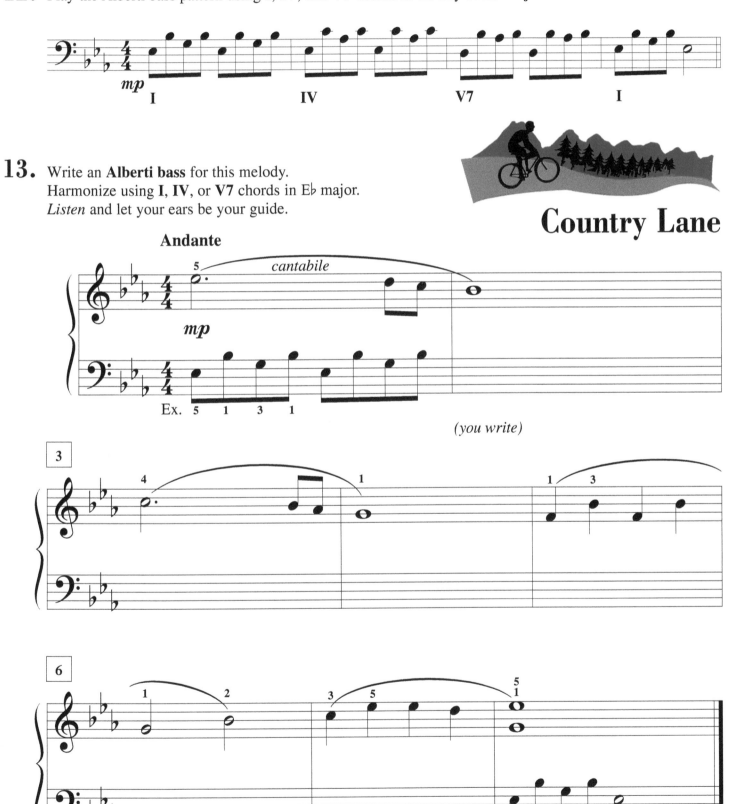

13. Write an **Alberti bass** for this melody.
Harmonize using **I**, **IV**, or **V7** chords in E♭ major.
Listen and let your ears be your guide.

Country Lane

(you write)

Extra Credit: Play *Country Lane* with a friend doubling the melody on flute, violin, or digital keyboard.

Lessons p. 42

14. **A melody will sometimes outline a chord.**

The melodies below are built on **chord tones.**

Study each, naming the chord and its starting note.
Then sightread and transpose to the key suggested.

Name the chord outlined. —— Does the melody begin on the **root**, **3rd**, or **5th**? *(circle)*

a.

Transpose to B♭ major.

Name the chord outlined. —— Does the melody begin on the **root**, **3rd**, or **5th**? *(circle)*

b.

Transpose to G major.

Name the chord outlined. —— Does the melody begin on the **root**, **3rd**, or **5th**? *(circle)*

c.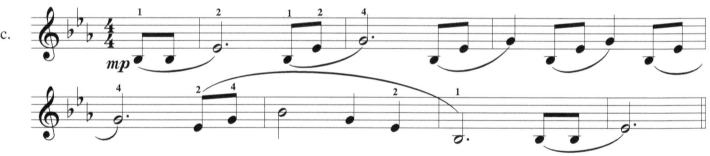

Transpose to D major.

15. Your teacher will play cadences in the key of E-flat.

Listen! Circle **I** or **V7** for the *last chord* you hear.

Remember, the **I** chord sounds *restful.* The V7 chord sounds *restless.*

       a. **I** or **V7**   b. **I** or **V7**   c. **I** or **V7**   d. **I** or **V7**

For Teacher Use Only (The examples may be played in any order and repeated several times.)

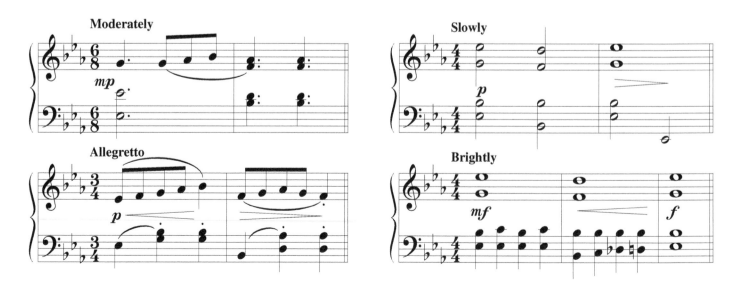

FF10

White Water Rafting
Down the D Minor River

1. Guide your "keyboard raft" down the "D Minor River" by completing each example.

You're off!

Avoid the boulder by writing the **key signature** for D minor.

Put an ✘ on the **raised 7th step** of the D harmonic minor scale.

Stop for a picnic and strum these **D minor chords** on your guitar.

Safely ride the current by writing the **D harmonic minor** scale. Include the correct flats and sharps.

root
position

1st
inversion

2nd
inversion

"Shoot the rapids" by writing the **D melodic minor** scale ascending and descending. Include all ♯'s, ♭'s, and ♮'s.

Give a camper directions by spelling the **minor iv chord** in the key of D minor.

____ ____ ____

Return home by writing the Roman numerals for this cadence.

(i, iv, or **V7)**

? ? ?

Fingering Adventures in D minor

In more advanced music, pianists are expected to write their *own* fingering in the music.

2. **Write your own fingering for this piece.**

Hint: Write in fingering whenever…

- the hand position changes
- the thumb passes-under or a finger crosses-over
- a fingering will help you see a pattern

Italian Dance

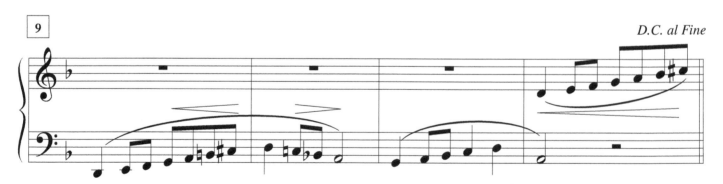

Which minor scale is this?
harmonic or *melodic?* (circle one)

Which minor scale is this?
harmonic or *melodic?* (circle one)

3. Have your teacher play *Italian Dance* using your fingering. How did your teacher do?

Relative Minor Review:

The *relative minor* key can be found by counting **down 3 half steps** from the *major* key.

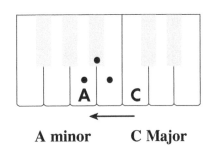

A minor   C Major

4. Each slice of pizza relates to the circle of 5ths. Observe the key signature for each "slice." Then name the **relative major** and **minor** keys in the pepperoni.

The Key Signature Pizza

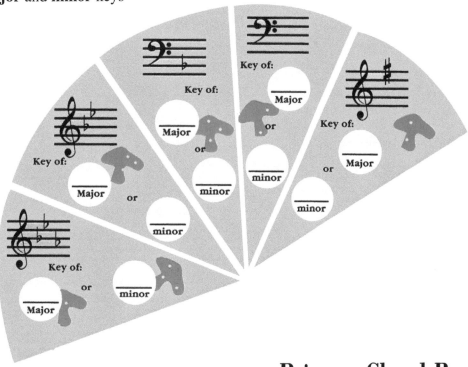

Primary Chord Review

5. Name the **tonic**, **subdominant**, and **dominant** triads for each major and minor key:

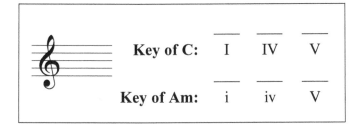

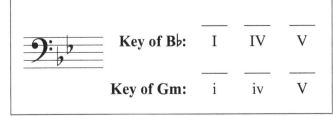

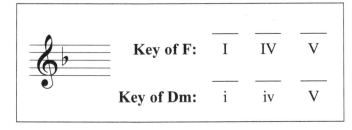

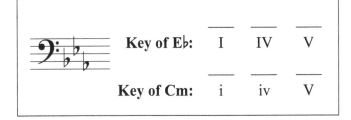

Chord Analysis

It is easier to play a piece by **recognizing chords** than by reading every individual note.

6. **Analyze** each measure by writing the chord letter name in the box given.

Then play the piece thinking "chords" rather than individual notes.

Enjoy using your knowledge of chords!

Rhythm Flight II

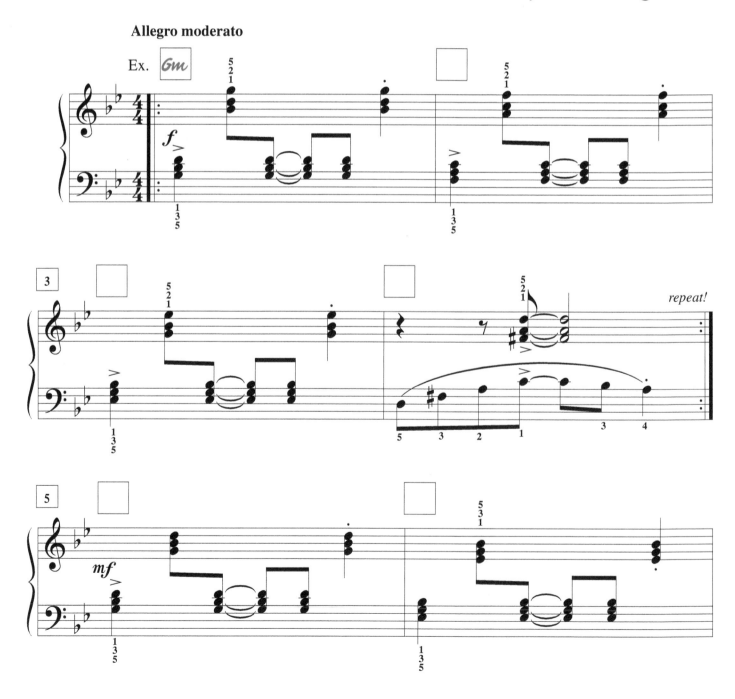

subito—means suddenly

Imagine a kitten has pounced on your piano keys!

Kitten on the Keys

(Chord Inversion Review)

7. Analyze the chord the kitten has played.
- First write the **chord letter name** in the box.
- Notice the key and circle **i**, **iv**, **V**, or **V7**.
- Then circle **root position**, **1st inversion**, or **2nd inversion**.

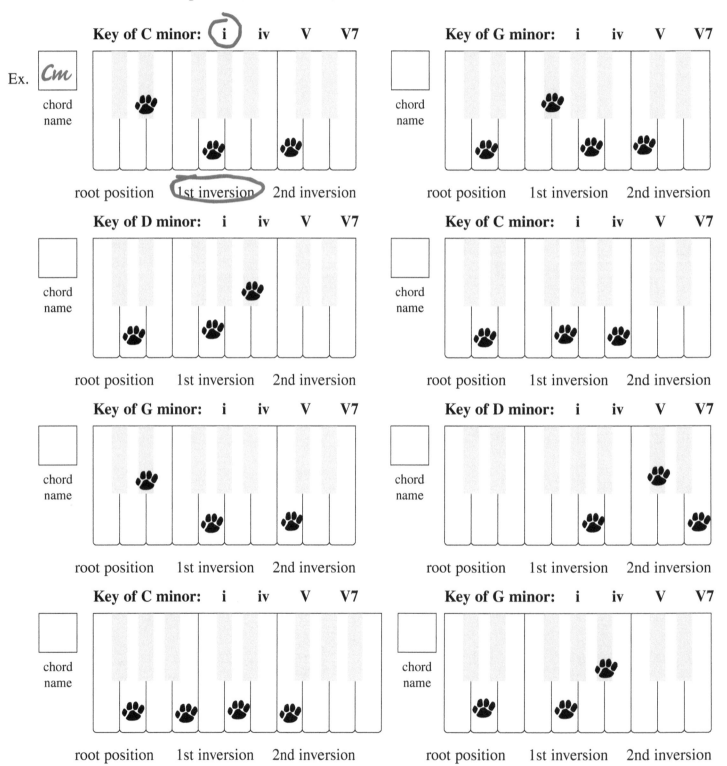

Extra Credit: Play **i**, **iv**, and **V** chords in **root position**, hands together, in these keys.

D minor   G minor   C minor

FF1

8. Analyze each example:

- Write in the **chord letter name** *above* the measure.
- Write the **Roman numeral** in the box *below* the measure.

Then sightread these melodies in minor keys.

Can you transpose to A minor?
(Hint: The R.H. begins in the 2nd inversion.)

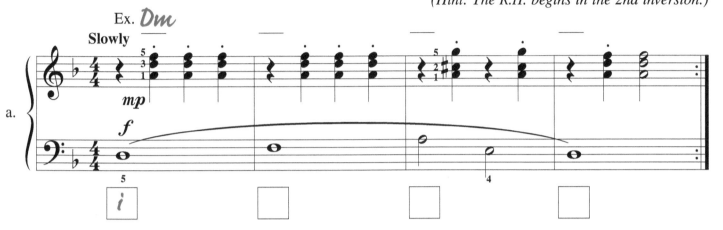

a.

Can you transpose to D minor?
(Which form of the minor scale is used?)

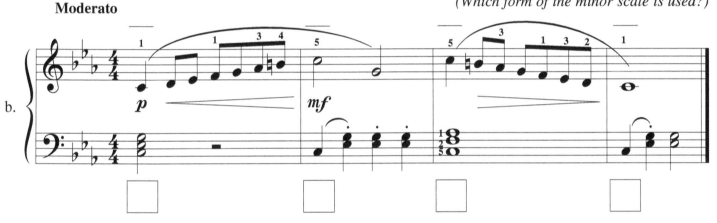

b.

9. Your teacher will play a minor scale.

Listen! Then circle **natural**, **harmonic**, or **melodic minor** for the scale that you hear.

1. natural minor?	2. natural minor?	3. natural minor?	4. natural minor?
harmonic minor?	harmonic minor?	harmonic minor?	harmonic minor?
melodic minor?	melodic minor?	melodic minor?	melodic minor?

For Teacher Use Only (The examples may be played in any order and repeated several times.)

Teacher Note: Continue the exercise playing other minor scales for the student to identify.

Lessons p. 53

Final Review (UNITS 1-6)

10. These pianos are awaiting inspection before going to the showroom.

- Send any pianos with **mistakes on their tags** back to the **factory**.
  (Draw a connecting line from the piano to the factory.)
  X-out and correct any false information.

- Send the pianos with **correct tags** to the **showroom**!
  (Draw a connecting line from the piano to the showroom.)

Piano Inspection

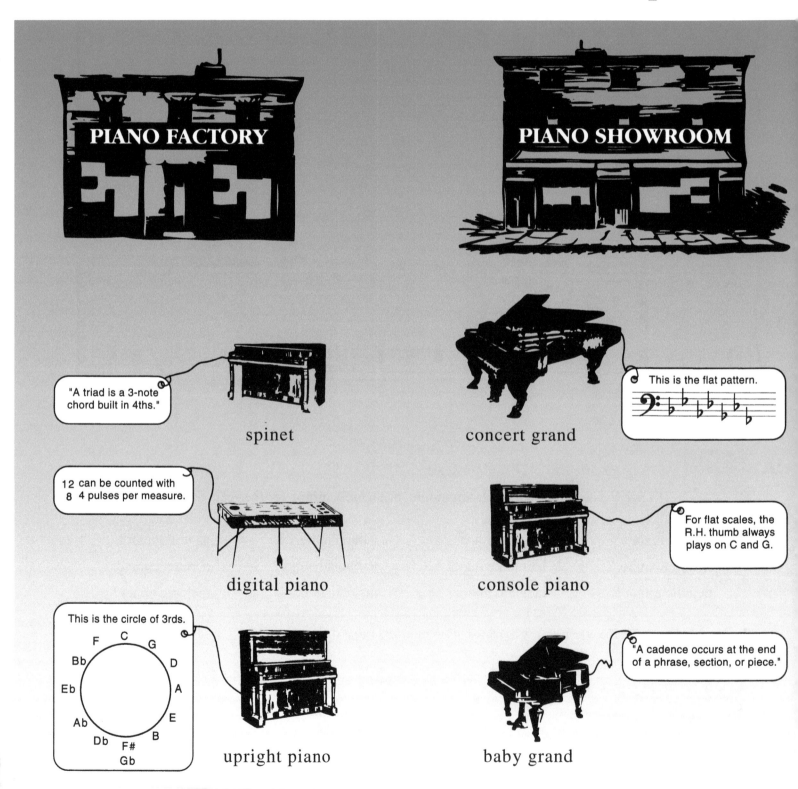

PIANO FACTORY

PIANO SHOWROOM

"A triad is a 3-note chord built in 4ths."

spinet

concert grand

This is the flat pattern.

12/8 can be counted with 4 pulses per measure.

digital piano

console piano

For flat scales, the R.H. thumb always plays on C and G.

This is the circle of 3rds.

F C G
Bb   D
Eb   A
Ab   E
  Db   B
  F#
  Gb

upright piano

baby grand

"A cadence occurs at the end of a phrase, section, or piece."

Congratulations! You've completed Level 5 Theory!